Looking at...

RACISM

Cath Senker

WAYLAND

First published in 2009 by Wayland

Copyright © Wayland 2009

Wayland
338 Euston Road
London NW1 3BH

Wayland Australia
Level 17/207 Kent Street
Sydney NSW 2000

Produced for Wayland by
White-Thomson Publishing Ltd

W!

+44 (0) 845 362 8240
www.wtpub.co.uk

Editors: Sonya Newland and Katie Powell
Designer: Robert Walster

British Library Cataloguing in Publication Data
Senker, Cath
    Looking at racism
    1. Racism - Juvenile literature
    I. Title II. Racism
    305.8

ISBN: 9780750258852

Picture Credits
AKG London: 16; Associated Press: 22 (Charles
Dharapak), 25 (Eddie Adams), 39; The Bridgeman
Art Library: 13; Camera Press: 8, 24, 34, 42; Corbis:
19 (Sion Touhig), 21 (Ralf-Finn Hestoft), 29 (Shawn
Thew/epa), 36 (Sandy Felsenthal); Howard J. Davies:
27; Paul Doyle: 4, 45; Getty Images: 30, 37, 38 (AFP),
44; Robert Harding Picture Library: 12; iStock: *cover*
(Dustin Steller); Panos Pictures: 6 (Betty Press), 28
(Betty Press), 33 (David Reed), 35 (Penny Tweedie);
Popperfoto: *contents* (bottom), 9 (Adrees Latif,
Reuters), 18 (Rula Halawani, Reuters), 23 (Mike Theiler,
Reuters), 40, 41 (Juda Ngwenya, Reuters), 43; Still
Pictures: 17 (Hartmut Schwarzbach); Topham
Picturepoint: *contents* (top), 5 (Jacksonville Journal
Courier/The Image Works), 7 (Adrian Murrell), 10, 11,
14, 15, 20, 26, 31 (Jeff Greenberg/The Image Works), 32.

The author would like to thank the following for their
help: Alison Brownlie; Michael Cardona; Ruth Cohen
for the case study in Chapter 5; Minority Rights Group
and Christiana Kwarteng for the case study and picture
in Chapter 6; Jill Rutter for permission to adapt part of
Refugees: A Resource Book for Primary Schools, 1998
for the case study in Chapter 4.

Every attempt has been made to clear copyright.
Should there be any inadvertent omission please
apply to the publisher for rectification.

Printed in China

Wayland is a division of Hachette Children's Books,
an Hachette UK company.
www.hachette.co.uk

CONTENTS

What is racism?

Some people think that humans can be divided into separate races. They believe that these races look different and have different characteristics, such as being clever or being good at sports.

Different races

These ideas about race became popular about 200 years ago. A man named Count Arthur Gobineau wrote that history was a struggle between three races: the yellow, the black and the white. He thought that the white race was better than the others. Even then, though, there were people who believed in only one race: the human race.

FACT

All the differences in skin colour in Europe and Africa are controlled by just six genes out of a total of 30,000 in the human body.

← Children become aware of ideas about race from an early age.

Skin colour

Scientists have now proved that there are not different races of people. The colour of someone's skin has always been seen as an important sign of their race. But in fact the genetic differences between so-called races – for example, black and white people – are smaller than the differences that can be found within one of these groups.

Yet there are many people who still believe there are different races. The idea of race still matters to society, even though science has proved it wrong.

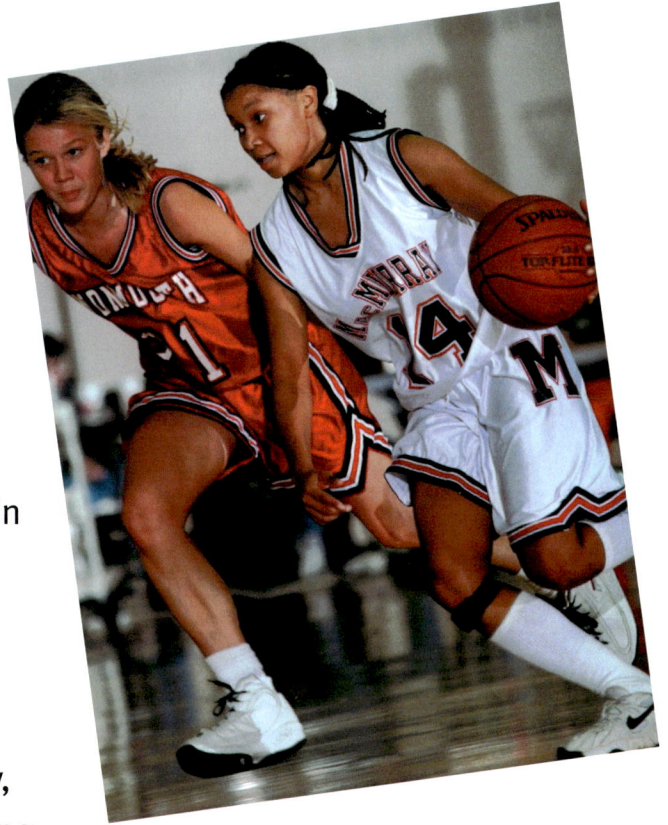

↑ These basketball players in the USA show that both black and white people can play the game.

'A white child said to his black schoolmate, "I wish I was black so I could play basketball as well as you." We often hear this kind of reasoning: "Everyone I see playing basketball is black. Everyone playing basketball must be black. If I am not black, I can't play basketball; if you are black, you must be a basketball player."'
Patricia Williams, Reith Lecturer

What is prejudice?

Thinking badly of a particular group without reason is called prejudice. To have a prejudice means to pre-judge someone – to make up your mind before you know anything about them.

People can be prejudiced for many reasons. For example, some people hate beggars on the street because they think they are too lazy to work. Some are prejudiced against people whose language or beliefs are different from their own.

⬇ Mixed black and white families may suffer from racism, which can make it hard for them to find a job and a home.

Why are people racist?

Being prejudiced against people because of their skin colour, ethnic group, religion or culture is called racism.

People can be racist towards others because of what they think they are like, even if it is not true. Some English people say the Irish are stupid, for example.

← Many Aborigines are so poor that they have to live in tin huts or shacks.

What is discrimination?

Sometimes people who suffer from racism are treated worse than others in society. In Australia, for example, Aborigines can find it hard to get into a good school or to find a decent job. They are more likely to be sent to prison for committing a crime. This is called discrimination.

Who are racists?

In most parts of the world, people do not like to be called racists – it is an insult. Yet racism exists all over the world. The racism of some white people against other groups is a problem, but non-white people can be racist, too.

'Article 2: Everyone should have the rights outlined in the Universal Declaration whatever their ethnic group, sex, nationality, religion, political opinion, social group, ability or wealth.'

THE UNIVERSAL DECLARATION OF HUMAN RIGHTS IN SIMPLE LANGUAGE

Jokes and name-calling

Racism appears in many different forms. Some people with racist views may keep them to themselves. Others might laugh at racist jokes and pass them on, but they do not believe they are doing any harm.

You might hear racist nicknames being used in the classroom. The people using them may think it is just a bit of fun. But it makes life unpleasant and can be frightening for the people who are being called names.

Harassment and violence

Some racists take action against the people they hate. Members of a white family who do not like their Asian neighbours may harass them. They might call the children names or post rubbish through the letterbox.

Refugees are people who leave their own country because they do not feel safe there. Some people do not like refugees. They may be violent towards them or attack a hostel where refugees live.

↑ In the 1970s, the racist National Front organized marches through black areas. Here they have destroyed Asian people's shops in East London.

Organized racism

In many countries there are racist political organizations that try to gain support for their ideas. The Ku Klux Klan is a racist group formed by white Americans in the nineteenth century. It still campaigns against African-Americans, Koreans and Jews.

In the worst cases, racist organizations may get into power and try to kill all the people in the group they hate. This is what happened under the Nazis during World War II.

'Three young skinheads drank vast quantities of alcohol, and roamed rowdily through the town's park. They hit the black African, Alberto Adriano, for such a long time that he died of severe injuries in hospital three days later.'

BREMER NACHRICHTEN (ADAPTED), 23 AUGUST 2000

⬇ Ku Klux Klan members calling for African-American Gary Graham to be executed for murder. Graham claimed he was innocent, but he was executed in June 2000.

Racism in history

There are lots of examples of prejudice throughout history. These prejudices were not always based on skin colour, but people were often prejudiced against foreigners and groups who led a different way of life.

Distrust of foreigners

People often did not trust visitors from other places, because their customs were different. People did not travel much, so even those from another part of the same country were thought of as 'foreigners'. There was certainly dislike of people from another country.

⬇ Romanies leaving Hurtwood Hill in Surrey, England, in 1934. They had been living in the settlement for 100 years.

Romanies

The Roma people (Gypsies), left India about 1,000 years ago and have moved around the world ever since. People often blamed them for crime, and used this as an excuse to attack them as 'outsiders'.

← A racist spraying a Nazi swastika on a wall in Belgrade, Serbia. Anti-Semitism can still be seen in many places.

Anti-Semitism

The Jewish people have suffered terrible racism for many centuries. When racism is directed against Jews it is called anti-Semitism.

Throughout history, Christian governments tried to make the Jews become Christians. They would only accept them if they gave up their religion. Jews sometimes suffered under Muslim rulers, and harsh laws were passed against them.

During the eighteenth and nineteenth centuries, these early forms of prejudice turned into a new kind of hatred based on ideas about 'race'.

FACT

In the Middle Ages, many Western European countries passed laws to throw out all Jewish people. Jews were forced out of England in 1290, France in 1394 and Spain in 1492.

'A HISTORICAL ATLAS OF THE JEWISH PEOPLE'.

Colonialism

Around 400 years ago, European nations sent ships and soldiers to other parts of the world. They began to rule over the countries they discovered. This was the beginning of colonialism, and it led to new ideas about 'race'.

Slavery

The colonists needed people to work on their farms, so they brought millions of African people as slaves. Africans were seen as no better than animals, or children who needed a firm hand.

FACT

About 12 million Africans were torn from their homes and taken across the Atlantic Ocean as slaves. More than one in 10 died on the way. Those who survived were sold and then forced to work up to 18 hours a day.

ROBIN BLACKBURN, 'THE MAKING OF NEW WORLD SLAVERY'.

← This painting shows slaves in North America. They look relaxed, but in fact their lives were extremely hard.

Racist attitudes towards natives

In countries such as South Africa, Europeans took control of the land and made local Africans work for them. Colonists also took over parts of Asia, Africa and South America. The Europeans thought the native peoples were not able to govern themselves.

Europeans also settled in places such as Australia, New Zealand and North America. They thought they were better than the native peoples. Some people still believe that white European people are better than everyone else.

⬇ A portrait of Olaudah Equiano. In England he joined the campaign against the slave trade.

CASE STUDY ▸ CASE STUDY ▸ CASE STUDY ▸

In 1756, aged 11, Olaudah Equiano was kidnapped from his village in Nigeria. An African blacksmith took him as a slave. Olaudah had several other African owners before being sent on a slave ship to Barbados in the Caribbean. He was then taken to Virginia, North America, and forced to work on a tobacco plantation. A naval captain bought him next, and he spent several years at sea.

In 1766, Equiano bought his freedom. He had many adventures while working as a sailor. In Italy he saw the volcano Vesuvius erupt, and he was shipwrecked in the Bahamas. Equiano later moved to England and wrote his autobiography.

Fascism

In the 1920s and 1930s some countries, including Italy, Spain and Germany, came under fascist rule. Fascists were governed by a powerful leader called a dictator, and they believed their country was superior to others. They discriminated against people from other countries or cultures, and they conquered other countries by force.

⬇ A Jewish man is being stopped by Nazi soldiers in Berlin, Germany, in 1933.

Nazi Germany

The Nazi government in Germany was the most racist of the fascist powers. Its leader, Adolf Hitler, believed that 'Aryans' – blue-eyed Germans and Scandinavians – were a superior race. He thought that other races, such as the Slavs (people from Eastern Europe) and Africans, were fit only to be slaves. The Nazis hated the Jews most of all.

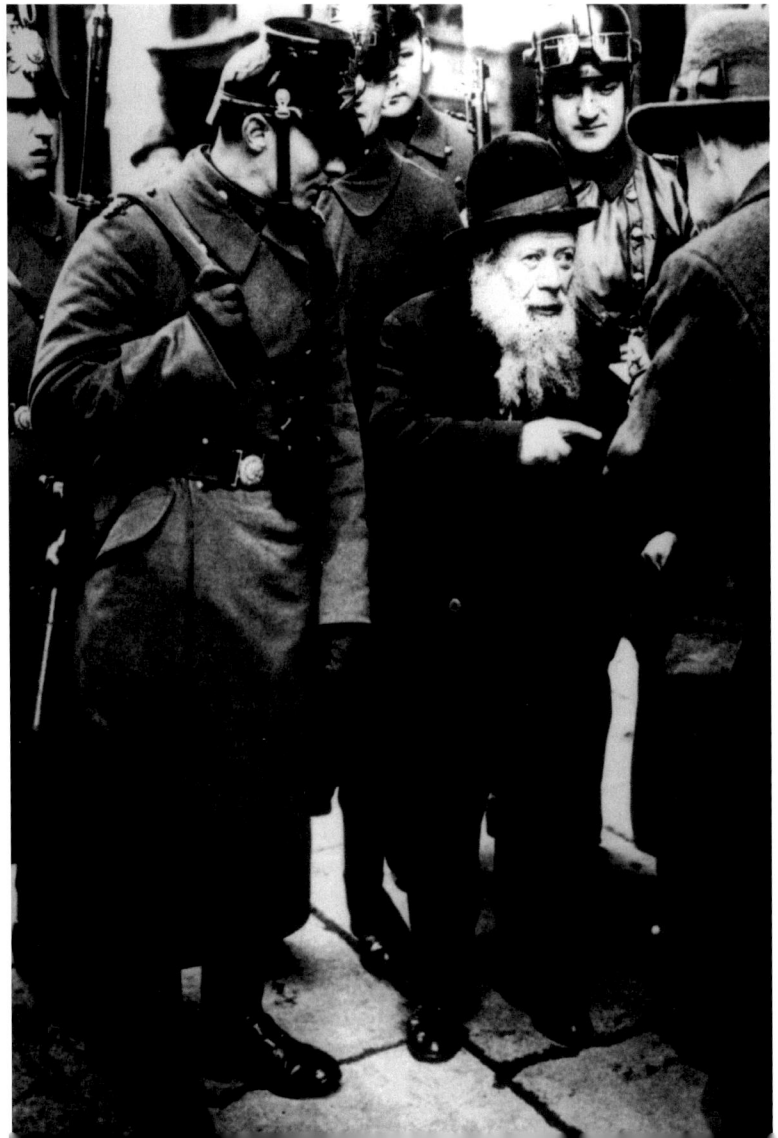

FACT

Millions of Jews in Eastern Europe were killed during World War II.

	Before the war	Jews killed
Poland	3,250,000	3,000,000
USSR	2,800,000	1,200,000
Romania	800,000	350,000
Hungary	400,000	300,000
Czechoslovakia	315,000	270,000

'A HISTORICAL ATLAS OF THE JEWISH PEOPLE'.

⬇ Two Jewish boys being shamed in their classroom in Nazi Germany in the 1930s. On the blackboard it says: 'The Jew is our greatest enemy. Beware of the Jew.'

Death camps

The Nazis built death camps, where they used poison gas to murder thousands of Jews every day. Millions of other people, such as Roma, Poles, Russians, homosexual people and disabled people, were also killed in these death camps.

Racism in other countries

There was a fascist party in Britain before World War II, too. In the USA, black and white people mostly lived separate lives. After the war, many people began to see that racism was wrong. But racist ideas did not go away completely.

Fear of the unknown

When people do not understand another country or culture, they may believe nasty ideas about it. They may think bad things about all the people who belong to that country or culture.

Stereotypes

The particular image you have of a whole group of people is a stereotype. People might be stereotyped because of the their age or sex. Stereotypes are usually insulting because you are not seeing a person as an individual.

Sometimes people are stereotyped because of their skin colour, culture or religion. Stereotypes suggest that something is true of a whole group of people, when it is not. For example, saying 'All Jews are rich' is a stereotype, because not all Jews are rich.

⬇ This poster shows a stereotype of a Jewish person, who is interested only in money.

DER ewige Jude

GROSSE POLITISCHE SCHAU IM BIBLIOTHEKSBAU DES DEUTSCHEN MUSEUMS
ZU MÜNCHEN · AB 8. NOVEMBER 1937 · TÄGLICH GEÖFFNET VON 10-21 UHR

Racism through ignorance

Racist ideas are often spread by untruths. White people may hear that Asians eat with their fingers. They may think this is a filthy habit. They do not know that picking up food with freshly washed fingers is a perfectly clean way to eat. It can be cleaner than eating with cutlery washed in a bowl full of dirty dishes!

Those people do not know this. They believe their own ways are better. They might pass on their stereotyped view of 'dirty Asians' to others. This is how racist ideas can spread.

⬆ A photo of Nairobi, Kenya, showing the city's modern office blocks and a wealthy Kenyan. This shows that the stereotype that all Kenyans are poor, is untrue.

'A class was shown a set of slides of Nairobi city centre, with its skyscrapers and modern office blocks. Yet when asked what they noticed, the first thing they mentioned was a beggar, hardly visible, in the corner.'

ANGELA GRUNSELL AND ROS WADE, 'MULTICULTURAL TEACHING TO COMBAT RACISM IN SCHOOL AND COMMUNITY'

Ethnic racism

Sometimes people are racist towards another ethnic group. For example, Chinese-Americans in the USA may speak their own language at home and follow Chinese customs. Some Americans may say that this group of people does not fit into their society.

Racism and religion

Racism is often linked to religion. For example, Muslim Asians in Western countries may suffer from 'double racism'. They are discriminated against because of the colour of their skin, and also because they practise Islam.

⬇ Muslims praying in Jerusalem. The conflict between Israelis and Palestinians is often seen as a cultural and religious battle between Judaism and Islam.

A Muslim family in London. People need to feel that they can dress according to their culture, without fear of being attacked for looking different.

Islamic stereotypes

People in Western countries may be afraid of Muslims who live there. Stereotypes about Islam are common. Some people believe it is a cruel religion. Others may think that all Muslims are terrorists. These myths can result in racist acts against Muslims.

Cultural differences

Many people do not say out loud that they hate other ethnic groups. Instead, they talk about cultural differences. Some people think that it is impossible for people from Western and non-Western cultures to live together.

'At school they would say, "Are you a terrorist?" And I would say, "No, I am from Libya," and they would say, "Yes, from Colonel Gaddafi," and I would say, "No, from Libya. He is just the president there."'
SARINA, 18

Suspicion of others

There are Roma communities in many parts of the world. They suffer from racism for different reasons. People are suspicious of them because they move around rather than living in one place. They have dark skin, and their own language and culture.

Roma stereotypes

There are lots of stereotypes about Roma people. They are often forced to camp in filthy places, so people say they are dirty. Some say they

FACT

There are thought to be around 15 million Roma people in the world, but it is hard to know whether this is accurate. When countries have official censuses, many Roma people lie about their ethnic origins because they are afraid people will discriminate against them if they know they are Roma.

⬇ An elderly Roma couple in Granada, Spain.

are criminals and cannot be trusted. Settled people do not want their children to mix with them. The Roma are rarely welcomed.

➡ Czech Romanies protesting against a wall built to separate them from other people.

CASE STUDY ▶ CASE STUDY ▶ CASE STUDY ▶ CASE STUDY ▶

Josef is a Roma refugee from Slovakia. His family were driven out of their country. In Slovakia, the Roma were blamed for crimes they did not commit. They were attacked by gangs of skinheads, helped by the police. The skinheads wore boots with black laces. If they had beaten up lots of Roma, they wore white laces instead, like a medal.

Josef was attacked one afternoon by a group of skinheads. A week later he saw the leader of the group in police uniform. He went to the police station and told the officers about this, but they did not investigate. Then the police called him in and questioned him about various crimes. They beat him up.

Josef fled to the UK. He now lives in Dover. Life is not easy for him and his family because many people in Dover are racist towards the Roma.

Scapegoating leads to racism

Sometimes groups of people are blamed for causing problems when they have done nothing wrong. This is called scapegoating. For example, asylum seekers may be moved into an area where there are not enough jobs. Local people may think that the newcomers will take the few jobs there are. People may develop racist attitudes towards the asylum seekers because of this.

Scapegoating in Southeast Asia

There are around 25 million Chinese people living in countries in Southeast Asia. In some places they have been scapegoated because governments fear they have too much economic power.

Sometimes racist policies have been directed against them. They have even been forced to leave their countries.

⬇ Rioters in Sumatra, Indonesia, burning motorcycles stolen from a shop owned by Chinese people.

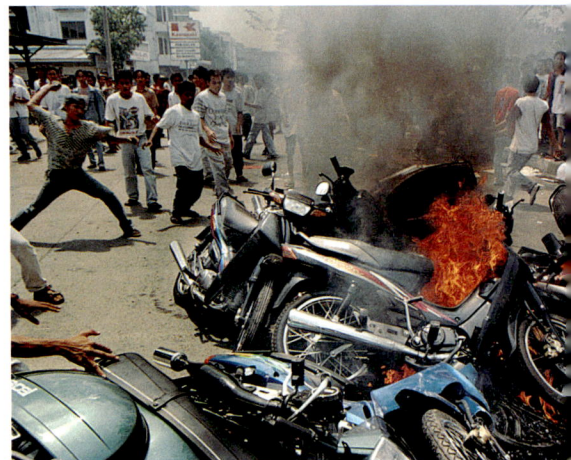

In Indonesia in 1998, Chinese people were blamed for the country's economic problems. Many of them were viciously attacked. Some were even killed.

'Maybe the separation [of the races] might be the best answer.'
LOUIS FARRAKHAN

Racism victims can be racist

People who suffer racism may scapegoat other groups. For example, Louis Farrakhan, leader of the African-American organization, The Nation of Islam, believes all white people are evil. He is also very anti-Semitic.

⬇ Although he has suffered racism, Louis Farrakhan hates white people and Jews, so he is a racist himself.

Asylum seekers

People may leave their own countries because
they have been attacked because of their
skin colour, culture, religion or political views.
They go to other countries where they hope to
be safe from discrimination. These people are
called 'asylum seekers'.

Life in a new country

Life can be difficult for asylum seekers in
their new country. Often they are not wanted.
They might be separated from the rest of the
population and made to live in hostels. They
may not be permitted to work. They may be
given coupons instead of money to buy food.

← A man being
arrested after an attack
on a hostel for refugees
in Rostock, Germany.

Racist attacks

Policies like this can lead to scapegoating. The new arrivals are seen as 'scroungers', getting something for nothing. There have been many racist attacks on refugee hostels. Sometimes racists even try to burn down buildings with the people still inside.

→ A Vietnamese woman and child fleeing Communist Vietnam on a fishing boat, 1977.

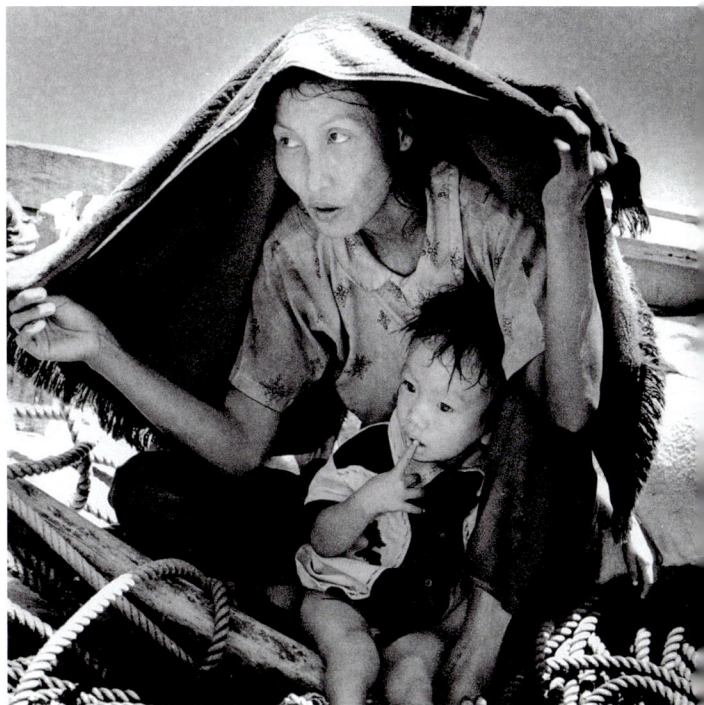

CASE STUDY ▸ CASE STUDY ▸ CASE STUDY ▸ CASE STUDY ▸

In 1978, Chinese people began to leave Vietnam after anti-Chinese racism increased. Most fled to other Southeast Asian countries. From 1979 to 1992, small numbers of Vietnamese refugees were allowed to enter Australia, Canada, the USA and Europe.

Quang Bui's brother escaped from Vietnam by boat. After a long and difficult journey, Quang Bui's brother reached Sweden and was allowed to settle there as a refugee. Quang Bui and his parents were later able to join him.

When he first arrived, Quang Bui was called 'yellow neck' and other racist names by older Swedish boys. But the Vietnamese kids stood up to them and nowadays everyone mixes together happily.

Racism and the media

The pictures we see in newspapers and on TV can affect the way we view people from other countries and cultures. Perhaps you only see Africans starving in poor villages. You may not know about the millions who live in flats or houses like you and go to work or school each day. This lack of information can lead to stereotyping of other peoples.

Stereotypes in films

For many years, films often presented a stereotyped view of black or Chinese people, for example. Black people were never shown as important, powerful or clever. The Chinese were portrayed as cruel people who could not be trusted.

There are now more black and Hispanic actors. African-American film director Spike Lee makes movies showing the problems of racism, and these are watched by people all over the world. They help break down racial stereotypes.

⬇ Spike Lee (left) has made many movies showing the lives of African-Americans. His work has encouraged black actors and directors.

Racist attacks by newspapers

Racism can still be found in the media, though. In many European countries, newspapers accuse asylum seekers of 'flooding' the country. They say the asylum seekers are making false claims. The newcomers are often accused of causing society's problems such as unemployment. Words written in the papers can encourage attacks on the streets.

⬆ Workers from the Refugee Arrivals Project at Heathrow Airport, England helping asylum seekers.

'German Jews pouring into this country

The way stateless Jews from Germany are pouring into this country is becoming an outrage.'

THE DAILY MAIL, 20 AUGUST 1938

'Revealed: How immigration could cause huge social problems

The economic tide is turning... The remarkable tolerance Britain has shown to these immigrants may be tested.'

THE MAIL ONLINE, 17 OCTOBER 2008

Institutional racism

Institutional racism is when society is organized in such a way that certain minorities are treated unfairly. In these societies, people from minorities may live in bad housing and have a poor education. This may mean they will only get low-paid jobs later in life.

Unequal treatment

In the USA, African-American and Hispanic people are not always treated in the same way as white Americans. This can make it difficult for them to improve their lives.

FACT

41.9 per cent of African-American children live below the poverty line.

INSTITUTE FOR JEWISH POLICY RESEARCH AND AMERICAN JEWISH COMMITTEE.

← Hispanic farm workers in the USA. These workers do not have the same rights as other workers in America.

CASE STUDY ▶ CASE STUDY ▶ CASE STUDY ▶ CASE STUDY ▶

It is hard to escape the effects of institutional racism, but music may offer a chance to Keisha, an African-American living in Chicago. Keisha was born a drug addict because her mother was one. Keisha went to live with her white grandmother. She started learning the viola at school when she was eight.

Keisha won a scholarship to the Merit Music Programme, an inner-city music centre. Music became the focus of her life. Although she was thrown out of secondary school because of bad behaviour, she carried on playing the viola. Keisha became one of the best students at Merit. She hopes to study music at university.

Suppose that a Hispanic woman from Pilsen, Chicago, who managed to get a university degree, applies for a good job and is called for interview. Her interviewer does not hate Hispanic people, but she feels that someone from Pilsen is unlikely to succeed.

The Hispanic woman is less likely to get the job than a white person. It will be hard to raise her family out of poverty. One in every three African-American families and one in four Hispanic families is poor.

⬇ Barack Obama was the first African-American to be elected US president, in 2008.

Racism against native peoples

In some countries native peoples face problems because their lands are run by other people who see them as inferior. It may be hard for them to find a good home and make a living in their own land.

'We were here first'

In the nineteenth century, Europeans took land from the Australian Aborigines. Native Americans in the USA were moved off their land so white people could settle there. In the twentieth century, a system of laws called apartheid was introduced in South Africa to discriminate against natives.

← Australian basketball player Patrick Mills was one of several Aboriginal athletes who took part in the 2008 Olympic Games.

⬇ A Maya teacher with students, Guatemala. There are now schools here that teach the Maya in their own language.

The Maya of Guatemala

The native Maya people of Guatemala in Central America were almost wiped out by Spanish invaders in the sixteenth century. They have remained at the bottom of Guatemalan society ever since. They no longer own much land and most of them live in poverty.

The Maya suffer institutional racism because of their low position in society. They are often ignored when they go to hospitals. People overcharge them in shops and on buses. They are always being told they are lazy and dirty.

'You can't teach the Indians anything. How many times have we tried to improve their way of life? They just won't change.'

TYPICAL COMMENT ABOUT THE MAYA, QUOTED BY THE MINORITY RIGHTS GROUP, UK

Racism in schools

Belonging to a group that suffers from racism can affect children at school. If they live in a poor area, they are less likely to get into a good school. They may find that the other children do not understand their culture. Teachers may have stereotyped views that mean they treat these children differently.

Children from ethnic-minority groups often do worse at school. White students often leave school when they are 16 or 18 with much better qualifications than black students.

⬇ In some Western countries, Muslims have set up their own schools so that their children do not suffer from racism.

Open racism

Children may also suffer from open racism. They may be bullied or even attacked at school. Muslim girls may be picked on because they wear headscarves. Mixed-race children may be bullied by both white and black children.

Sometimes white children have been attacked in revenge for attacks on non-whites. White children may also suffer racist abuse if they have non-white friends.

Addressing the problem

Teachers and students are often aware of the problems of racism. They try to deal with racist behaviour. It helps if the school teaches children about the different cultures in society and how to respect them all.

➜ Children at Alexandria Park primary school in Zimbabwe, where black and white students are taught together.

FACT

In the USA, almost two-thirds of money given to students to help them to go to university is in the form of loans – money to be paid back. In general, white students will borrow money to pay to go to a good university. They believe they will be able to pay it back when they get a good job. Black students usually worry about borrowing a lot of money, so they tend to go to lower-grade universities.

DEREK PRICE, SOCIOLOGIST.

Feeling superior

Many people feel proud of their country, its history and culture. It is good to be proud of your country, but some extreme nationalists may believe that only people born in their country have a right to live there. They feel superior to the newcomers.

Racism against immigrants

This feeling is more common if the new arrivals come from a different ethnic group or culture. It can lead to racist attitudes towards them. White people from Australia or South Africa usually find it easy to settle in Europe. Yet Afro-Caribbean, African and Asian immigrants have suffered from racism.

➡ A crowd waving American flags in New York. Nationalism can bring people together, but it can also turn them against outsiders.

Fitting in

Even minorities who have lived in another country for a long time may experience racism. For example, Korean people in Japan suffer discrimination in housing and jobs, even if they have lived there all their lives. Many Japanese feel superior to the Koreans and think that they simply do not fit into their society.

'Many sangokujin [third-world people] and other foreigners who have entered Japan illegally have repeatedly committed atrocious crimes. In the event of a major earthquake, riots may break out.'

TOKYO GOVERNOR SHINTARO ISHIHARA

'One true culture'

Most countries are made up of a mixture of different cultures, ethnic groups and religions. But racists often believe that their country has only one true culture. They think that foreigners spoil this and bring problems to the country.

⬇ Many Filipinos work as servants in countries in the Middle East to make money to send home to their families.

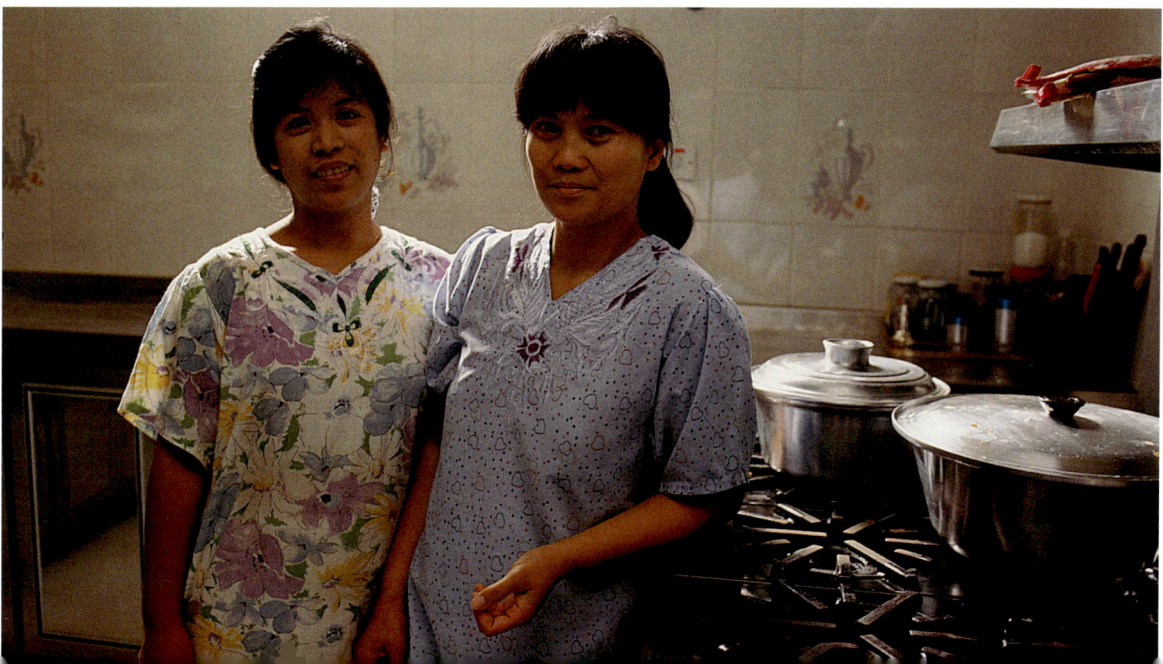

'We're better than you'

Many people move to another country because they think they can earn more money there. Immigrants often move from poorer countries to richer ones.

Immigrants often take the badly paid jobs that no one else wants. When they see immigrants sweeping the streets or cleaning toilets, some people may feel they are superior. In this way racist views can start to spread.

FACT

Many countries are made of of lots of different ethnic groups. In 2006, the population of the USA was about 299 million. This included:
Whites: 198.1 million
African-Americans: 40.9 million
Hispanics: 44.3 million
Asians: 13.1 million
Native Americans:
2.0 million

← Many people whose families come from Mexico live in San Antonio, in the USA, so a lot of the shops there sell Mexican food.

Taking over society

Out of 100 million Mexicans, around 40 million live in poverty. About seven million of them live in the USA. Some white Americans feel that Mexican customs and language are 'swamping' their country. This can lead to racism against Mexicans.

⬇ These IT specialists in Bangalore, India, may one day work in Europe or the USA, as their skills are recognized abroad.

The value of immigrants

The US and European economies need well-qualified immigrants. Yet some people find it hard to accept even skilled newcomers who are valuable to society.

CASE STUDY ▸ CASE STUDY ▸ CASE STUDY ▸

Christiana Kwarteng came to the Netherlands from Ghana. Before she arrived, she thought that all Dutch people were blond and friendly. She believed that they lived freely and were rich. She thought it would be hard to find work there.

Christiana found that it was indeed hard to find a job. But she saw that only some people had blond hair, and not everyone was friendly. Some people were racist and discriminated against her. Also, young people had little respect for the elderly, which she felt was wrong. Some things were better in the Netherlands, but she didn't find that all European ways were superior.

Fascism rears its ugly head

After the horrors of World War II, it might seem strange that there are still fascists. But there will always be some people who feel that they are better than other ethnic groups. Fascist organizations still exist in places such as Europe, the USA, South Africa and India.

'I do not know one person in the National Front who committed even the most minor hostile act against a Jewish person.'

FRENCH NATIONAL FRONT LEADER JEAN-MARIE LE PEN

Fascism in Europe

Fascist parties have gained some political power in European countries, including the fascist British National Party in the UK. Fascists talk about protecting their national culture. They suggest that poverty is caused by immigrants. They think money should be spent on local people – meaning white people. They blame immigrants for problems in society.

← Jean-Marie Le Pen is the leader of the National Front fascist party in France.

Fascism in the USA

In the USA there are small fascist groups. They do not have political power, but they are active in other ways. They attack African-Americans, Jews, Koreans and homosexual people. They set fire to their homes or vandalize their property.

Fascism in India

In India, the Bharatiya Janata Party (BJP) believes Hinduism is the true religion. It wants to force the country to accept Hindu laws, although 100 million Indians are Muslim. In states where it has been elected, the BJP has scapegoated Muslims. In Mumbai, Bangladeshi Muslims have suffered beatings by the police. Many have been sent back to Bangladesh.

← Muslims have tied a Hindu man to a handcart and are pulling him through the streets during a riot in Mumbai, India.

What can we do?

Throughout history, wherever there has been racism, there have always been people who have fought against it.

The civil rights movement

African-Americans were not treated equally in the USA even after slavery ended in 1865. They were paid lower wages and had poorer homes and schools. In the 1960s, many black and white people joined the civil rights movement. They held marches and campaigns, hoping to make the government change the laws so that black people were treated equally.

⬇ The Reverend Martin Luther King, one of the main leaders of the US civil rights movement.

FACT

Montgomery, Alabama, 1955: Rosa Parks, an African-American woman tired after her day's work, sat down in the only remaining seat – in the whites-only part of the bus. A white man demanded to sit down but she refused to get up. This sparked the Montgomery bus boycott, and the start of the US civil rights movement.

Apartheid

In 1948, the South African government brought in the apartheid system. This divided its people into separate 'races'. White people had most rights and black Africans the fewest. Black people could not mix with white people. They had separate schools, buses and even park benches. Most lived in poverty.

Many ordinary people from all over the world supported the campaign against apartheid. In the eary 1990s, apartheid was finally banned in South Africa. The country elected its first black president, Nelson Mandela.

⬆ Nelson Mandela was the first black president of South Africa. He served from 1994 to 1999.

Civil rights in Australia

In the 1960s, Australian Aborigines started their own civil rights movement. They took a new pride in their Aboriginal lifestyle and culture. They wanted to win back the land that was taken from them by the Europeans. Finally, in 1993, Aborigines began to recover their land.

Taking a stand

Stopping racism is not always a huge struggle against a political power like the apartheid government in South Africa. Often it is a matter of stopping a few people before they grow powerful. Everyone can take a stand.

Organizing and protesting

Some people will take to the streets to protest against racism. In Austria, many people were shocked when Jörg Haider, leader of the fascist Freedom Party, came second in the national elections in 1999. Thousands of Austrians protested against Haider's party. They were afraid that if the party came to power, there would be more racism in their country. Haider died in 2008, but the party still exists.

◄ A demonstration following the election of Jörg Haider in Austria. The middle poster says 'Fascism never again'.

⬇ Rodney King was beaten by white policemen in Los Angeles, USA in 1992. The policemen weren't convicted, which sparked riots in the city.

'You have to take a stand against racism.'
REGINA HORST

'[I came] to make a symbolic gesture and try to give another picture of Germany.'
FLAVIA-VICTORIA MAI

SUPPORTERS OF AN ANTI-NAZI DEMONSTRATION OF ABOUT 200,000 PEOPLE IN BERLIN, GERMANY, NOVEMBER 2000

The murder of Stephen Lawrence

Most British people were shocked by the murder of black teenager Stephen Lawrence in London in 1993. The police did not arrest the suspects, even though they had information about a gang of five racists who carried knives and boasted about using them on black people.

Stephen's parents kept pushing the police to find their son's killers. Ordinary people around the country supported their efforts. Later, an official inquiry found that there was institutional racism in the police force, which had not worked hard enough to find Stephen's killers.

43

How can we help?

If you hear racist remarks or jokes, or if there is racist bullying at your school, you can try doing some or all of these things:

• Speak out. If you say nothing, others may think you agree.

• Invite speakers from different communities to help to break down prejudice ideas.

• Organize discussions about human rights and racism.

• Form a school policy against racism.

• Join an anti-racist or human rights organization.

'The media have a big say in how asylum seekers are treated... Maybe one day they can change it around and be on our side and prove that racism isn't good.'

ASHLEY COLE, PROFESSIONAL FOOTBALLER

⬇ Ashley Cole, football player for England. Success in sport can be a good way of breaking down racial prejudices.

Taking responsibility

It is up to all of us to do what we can. We would all be happier in a society free from the fear, distrust, ignorance and prejudice that cause racism.

➡ Having friends from different cultures makes life richer and more interesting.

CASE STUDY ▸ CASE STUDY ▸ CASE STUDY ▸ CASE STUDY ▸

Mary Seacole Comprehensive Girls' School in the Midlands, England, has students from many backgrounds. Just under half are from South Asian families, a third are white, and about 18 per cent are Afro-Caribbean. To tackle the problem of racism, the students were involved in making an anti-racist policy. Some of the teachers weren't keen at first, but the girls' enthusiasm persuaded them that change was needed.

Now, the students often deal with racist incidents themselves. As one girl says, 'We find if people are racist that the person [making the comments] is isolated. You know, even their own friends will isolate that person.' Most of the white girls take the issue just as seriously. All the girls talk about the benefits of knowing people from different cultures and religions.

GLOSSARY

Anti-Semitism
Hatred of Jewish people.

Apartheid
A system brought in by the white South African government in 1948. It kept white, black and mixed-race people separate and unequal.

Asylum
The right to live in another country if you are under attack in your own. People who flee to other countries because of this are called asylum seekers.

Boycott
To get together with other people to refuse to have anything to do with a group of people, or foreign country.

Civil rights
The rights of people in a country to live freely and equally, whatever their ethnic group or personal views.

Colonialism
When one country rules another land as if it owned it.

Discrimination
Treating a group of people worse than other groups.

Ethnic group
A group of people who share a common culture, tradition and perhaps language.

Ethnic minority
A group who have a different culture, religion, language or skin colour from most other people in their society.

Fascism
An extreme right-wing system of government based on the belief that one country or ethnic group is better than all others.

Fascist
A person who believes that their country or ethnic group is better than all others, and obeys a powerful leader.

Genetics
The study of how physical features are passed on from parents to their offspring.

Harass
To keep troubling and annoying someone.

Hispanics
Spanish-speaking people living in the USA, whose families come from Latin America.

Ignorance
Not knowing about a subject.

Immigrants
People who enter another country to live there.

Ku Klux Klan
An extreme right-wing secret society, founded in the southern states of the USA in the 1860s to oppose giving rights to black people. It still exists today.

Nationalist
Someone who is very proud of their country and its culture.

Nazis
Supporters of Adolf Hitler's Nazi Party in Germany in the 1930s and 1940s.

Refugee
Someone who has moved to another country because they no longer feel safe in their own country, perhaps because of war or religious persecution.

Stereotype
Something that is said about a whole group of people. A stereotype is not based on fact and is insulting. It means people from that group are not seen as individuals.

Vandalize
To damage or destroy buildings deliberately.

FURTHER INFORMATION

ORGANIZATIONS

Australia & New Zealand
ACT Human Rights Office
GPO Box 158
Canberra, ACT 2601, Australia
Tel: (02) 6205 2222
www.hrc.act.gov.au

Commonwealth Human Rights
Equal Opportunity Commission
GPO Box 5218
Sydney, NSW 2000, Australia
Tel: (02) 9284 9600
www.hreoc.gov.au

Human Rights Commission of NZ
PO Box 6751
Wellesley Street, Auckland 1141
Tel: 0800 496 877
www.hrc.co.nz/home/default.php

South Australian Equal
Opportunity Commission
GPO Box 464
Adelaide, SA 5001, Australia
Tel: (02) 8207 1977
www.eoc.sa.gov.au

Europe
SOS Racisme
51 avenue de Flandre
Paris 75019, France
Tel: (01) 40 36 74 10
www.sos-racisme.org

EAFORD (International
Organization for the Elimination of
All Forms of Racial Discrimination)
5 Route des Morillons
Case Postale 2100
1211 Geneva 2, Switzerland
Tel: (022) 788 62 33
www.eaford.org

UK
Equality and Human
Rights Commission
3 More London
Riverside Tooley Street
London SE1 2RG
Tel: 020 3117 0235
Helpline: 0845 604 6610
www.equalityhumanrights.com

Institute of Race Relations
2–6 Leeke Street
King's Cross Road
London WC1X 9HS
Tel: 020 7833 2010
www.irr.org.uk

Minority Rights Group
54 Commercial Street
London E1 6LT
Tel: 020 7422 4200
www.minorityrights.org

The Runnymede Trust
7 Plough Yard, Shoreditch
London EC2A 3LP
Tel: 020 7377 9222
www.runnymedetrust.org

USA
Inter-American Commission
on Human Rights
1889 F St., NW,
Washington, D.C., 20006
Tel: (202) 458 6002
www.cidh.org

FURTHER READING

Talk About: Racism
by Cath Senker
(Wayland, 2008)

21st Century Debates: Racism
by Cath Senker
(Wayland, 2008)

Talking About Myself: Racism
by Angela Neustatter
(Franklin Watts, 2008)

INDEX